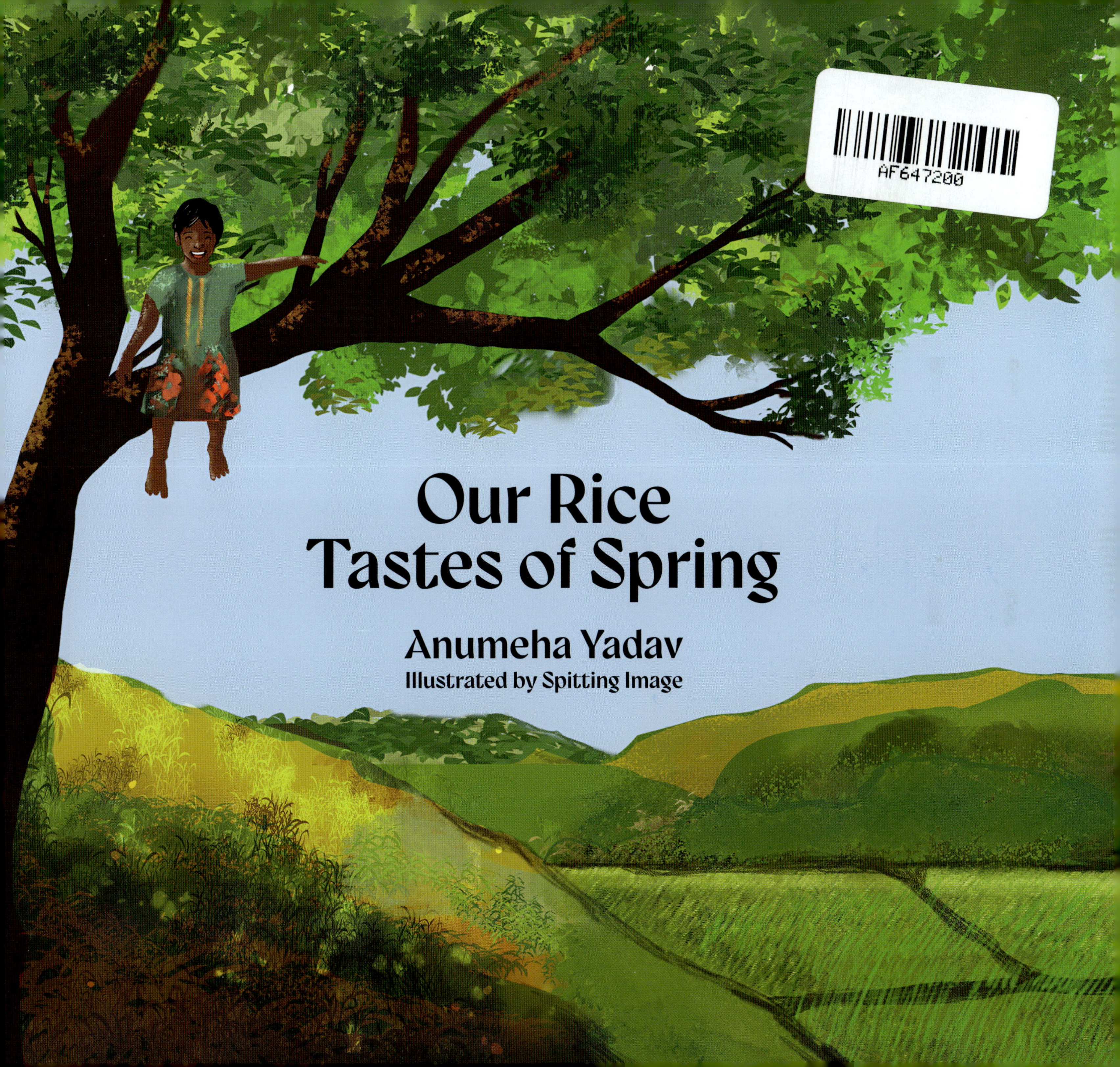

Our Rice Tastes of Spring

Anumeha Yadav

Illustrated by Spitting Image

Published by Red Panda, an imprint of Westland Books, a division of Nasadiya Technologies Private Limited, in 2025

No. 269/2B, First Floor, 'Irai Arul', Vimalraj Street, Nethaji Nagar, Alapakkam Main Road, Maduravoyal, Chennai 600095

Westland, the Westland logo, Red Panda and the Red Panda logo are the trademarks of Nasadiya Technologies Private Limited, or its affiliates.

ISBN: 9789360453145

10 9 8 7 6 5 4 3 2 1

Design: Spitting Image (Sandhya Visvanathan, Aniruddh Menon, Shoumik Biswas and Aditya Bharadwaj)

Rice photographs: Anupam Paul

Printed at Thomson Press (India) Ltd

To Helena, Ignacia, Anupa—for love and laughter,
for their struggles in Netarhat's present and past.

We are grateful to Budhaditya Bhattacharya, Parvati Sharma, Madhu Ramnath, Magdali Toppo, Shri Prakash, Soumik Banerjee, Veronica Dungdung and the residents of villages Chorha and Chormunda, Latehar for their thoughtful suggestions.

Early morning, the clucking of hens and the *dhundhuk-dhuk dhundhuk-dhuk* beat of the rhythmic pounding of rice in a *dheki* fills Jinid's home.

Jinid's village of Sohar, in Jharkhand's Chotanagpur region, has many kinds of rice and grains. In a corner of her house is the wooden pounder, a *dheki*, which her mother uses to turn paddy into rice—ready to cook and eat. Paddy is the whole grain still inside a protective cover.

Mother presses on the *dheki* repeatedly, in a rhythm. She pounds the paddy, so that the husk, which is the outer layer, loosens. She then tosses it lightly, winnowing it, until the husk and any dirt come off. Jinid and her cousins wait eagerly to eat.

'Jinid, this is Ranikajal rice. The plant will sprout tiny grains, which we make into flour to make *arsaa*, your favourite sweet on festivals, and my *hadiya* (fermented rice drink)' Jinid's grandfather tells her.

'Who named this rice "Ranikajal"? Did the kings and queens name them?' Jinid wants to know.

‘Our ancestors named the seeds. Ancient cultivators carefully chose the best seeds from the rice that grew in the wild. They created a treasure trove of rice varieties.’

'Our elders observed the plant's flowering time, leaves, stem, the colour and shape of various rice grains. They experimented and found out which rice grows best in the *doin* and in the *taand*. The *doin* is the wetland, a low-lying flat and muddy land, where we plant rice in water. The *taand* is high and drier land, where we grow rice using rainwater,' Grandfather explains.

‘Now, we know that the *doin* gives us many kinds of rice, like Jeeraphool, Kanakchampa, Sonpiya, Kalamdaani and many more,’ Grandmother adds.

‘In the *taand*, we plant seeds that can survive in less water, in case the rains arrive as scattered showers,’ states Grandfather.

'We have rice that can live submerged in water for days. The wondrous Lakshmi Dighal and Jabra rice can elongate their stems as floodwaters rise. Matla and Getu rice can tolerate salty soil, survive even a cyclone and provide food.'

'We can grow black rice, purple rice, red rice like the Hardiguda, Bhutmuri, medicinal rice like the Koronga, and so many other fragrant rice varieties.'

‘The seeds provide grains for us and the birds. The leaves and tall stalks become food for the animals. And the roots nurture the worms in the soil. In the monsoon, we harvest and eat fish and small crabs from the paddy wetlands. Later, we use paddy straw to grow more food, such as mushrooms,’ Grandmother tells Jinid.

Jinid's family don't need to buy anything to grow their rice. They have seeds and water, from the skies above.

'Noichi-dhaan is so fresh and delicious!' Jinid exclaims.

'Yes. Doesn't it taste like spring?' Her aunt smiles.

'Sahiya didi (government health worker) says rice provides starch and calories. But it is more than that. It is a source of life,' says Grandmother.

REVOLUTION RICE
PADDY+
PPP

One morning, an assembly is called. A strange man dressed in dark clothes and shoes arrives in the village. Jinid has never seen anyone like him. He is called the GainsMan.

'All of you grow rice, but what do you earn?' the man asks. 'Are you able to sell the rice? Why do you grow so many varieties when you know you cannot sell them all?'

GainsMan holds two packets in his hands, one smaller and one larger. He holds out some seeds from the smaller packet, 'See, these seeds will produce Revolution Rice, which is uniform and easy to sell.'

Holding up the other packet, he says, 'This large packet contains powdered petrol for plants (PPP), which is applied to the roots.'

All those gathered listen to him and take the new seeds and the 'PPP' into their homes and fields. Soon, the uniform-looking Revolution Rice replaces the earlier traditional folk rice varieties. The older seed varieties become hard to find, and the aroma and vivid colours of rice grains begin to disappear.

'Where have our own seeds disappeared, those that grew on *doin-taand* undulating lands like ours?' Grandfather asks.

The problem is not only the appearance. Grandfather says the new rice makes his body feel different. 'Eating these grains doesn't give me the strength and stamina to work in the fields all day.'

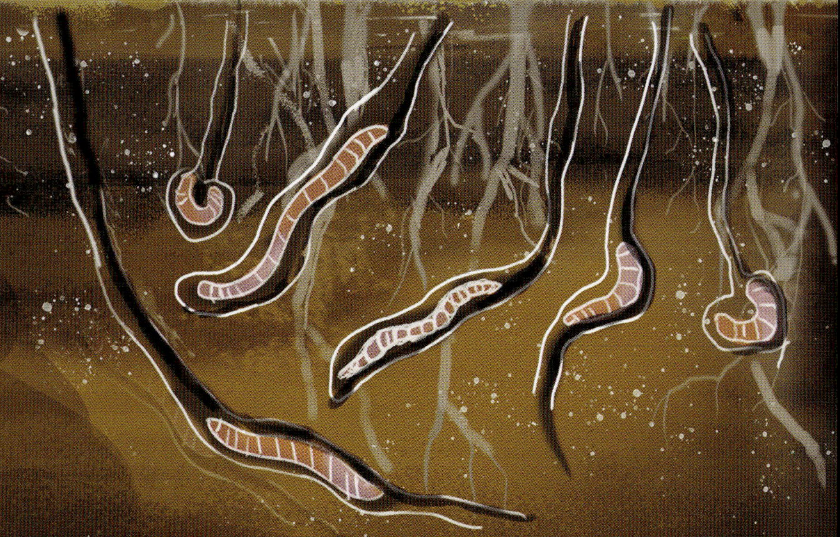

The powdered petrol for plants (PPP) collects in the shallow waters above the soil, killing the fish and small crabs which Jinid's family used to eat with rice. It slowly seeps in and poisons the worms that keep the earth healthy.

Jinid's family and neighbours watch as Revolution Rice and PPP bring growing destruction. The earth they grew their food on, the insects, worms and birds—all are affected.

Grandmother, too, isn't convinced by the new rice. 'This so-called Revolution Rice has none of the taste, aroma, colour or uniqueness our rice has.'

She notices that even the hens and pigeons do not eat the new grains. 'How can we trust it, when birds don't?'

Without listening to the village's questions or concerns, GainsMan returns with a new product.

'We have invented a formula for rice powder in our factories,' he declares. 'We pass a paste through a pasta machine to make artificial grains. It will be the whitest rice you have ever seen.'

This time, the villages remain quiet and do not respond immediately. Over several days, the people gather. Many conversations take place.

A few weeks later, Jinid watches as GainsMan brings a new packet to the village assembly. ‘This will bring back your stamina and cure your sickness. We can make it in our machines, so you no longer have to plant or grow anything!’

This time, when GainsMan presents the new Revolution packet, the entire assembly protests. They speak up in one voice: ‘Our seeds protect us. They are the source of the rhythm and strength of our everyday lives.’

Back home, Jinid's mother holds the older grains—red, brown, purple and black.

She has saved several kinds of the older seeds—the ones she uses for Jinid's *arsaa* sweets, Noichi-dhaan, the ones whose aroma she likes most, the ones Jinid's grandparents grow in the dry years, and those planted in the fields on top of the plateau.

'Our rice, cooking in our own way, with our tools and time, is important. For centuries, our grains have given life—not just to us, but to everything around us,' says Jinid's mother.

Grandmother agrees, 'The question a farmer growing our seeds faces is, what are you earning by growing the old rice?'

She adds, 'But livelihoods are not about that alone, are they? Our way of life is to be there during each other's *dukh-sukh* and to be one with our environment.'

Grandfather promises, ‘Our elders taught us how to care for our land—to eat in a way that keeps the trees and insects alive and to live in a way that protects the plants and soil. We grow more than twelve kinds of rice in our fields, and we will keep them alive.’

A few

Local Rice Varieties

from India's eastern region

Lakshmi dighal, Ranikajal and Jabra

Can survive a lot of rains by growing longer stems as floodwaters rise

Hardiguda, Bhutmuri and Koronga

Iron-rich red rice served to pregnant women

Matla, Getu and Kallurundai

Can grow on weathered soil, survive rising seawater

Dahar Nagra, Nalpai and Moul

Best known for making the famed *moori* or crisped rice

Kalamaliphool, Bahalguda, Lusri and Luhini

Grown in upland *taand* areas where they can survive with very little rain

Garib-Sal

Medicinal rice variety, rich in natural minerals, used to treat stomach infections

Jeeraphool and Sonpiya

Doin lowlands rice which naturally tolerate certain pests and diseases

Kanakchampa and Kalamdaani

Doin varieties, planted on land where water collects over many days

Agni-sal

Bright red grain, named Agni after 'fire', with a strong stem to resist storms and even cyclones.
Rich in iron and antioxidants

Afterword

I first worked in Jharkhand fourteen years ago, when I moved to Ranchi as a newspaper correspondent. My reporting focussed on certain destructive processes unfolding in the Chotanagpur region, India's mining heartland. Several villages laboured resiliently to safeguard *jal, jangal, zameen*—water, forests and lands—which deeply intertwine with their lives. I documented intense struggles as the people resisted dispossession from their means of subsistence, systems of knowledge and decision-making.

After leaving Ranchi, I went back to live in one Adivasi hamlet on the Netarhat plateau. It let me build relationships with a few families and elders and have slower, deeper conversations—experiences which shaped this story. I witnessed how even as every day brought new pressures and uncertainty, there was still plenty of gathering, collaborating and celebrating the precious natural beauty around us.

Does a new food policy really address hunger and disease? How should we grow our food in a way that respects our environment? Seeking answers, I returned to Jharkhand and Odisha and conducted interviews with residents of several villages—the 'people of rice'. These conversations became a series of stories on food policy in 2023-24, published in *TheWire.in.* A certain extractivism hollows out the soil, depletes our plates and food. Yet the memory of older seeds has remained—of every village having, as one older cultivator described, distinct rice varieties, fragrant and fresh like the spring.

Becoming a parent brought a new perspective. The idea of transforming the stories into a picture book began with an urge to recount the story in a format everyone, including the village communities and younger people, might experience and enjoy. Collaborating with Sandhya Visvanathan, Aniruddh Menon and the rest of the art collective Spitting Image, has brought the story of one such community to life.

I hope the trip to this lively village on the plateau becomes an invitation to recall, to re-enchant the world and make it new.

- Anumeha Yadav

Anumeha Yadav

Anumeha Yadav reports on labour and social policy. Her articles often highlight the effects of government initiatives on village and forest communities and those who migrate to work in cities.
She has reported for national dailies, such as *The Hindu* as its Jharkhand correspondent, *The Indian Express* and *Scroll.in*. Her favourite thing is to ride a two-wheeler under the sal trees in Latehar, Jharkhand.

Website:
thiscorrespondence.wordpress.com

Email: anumeha@protonmail.com

Spitting Image

Spitting Image is an animation and design studio based in Bangalore, run by Sandhya Visvanathan, Aniruddh Menon and Shoumik Biswas. They are friends who all love making art and music, and that's what brought them together.
Their previous work includes animated historical fiction, an interactive workbook for socio-legal research, identity design for multiple film festivals and a slew of commercial design projects. They enjoy collaborating with researchers to create engaging and visually striking visuals to communicate research to the public.

Website: spittingimage.in

Email: info@sptimg.in